COURAGEOUS HISTORY MAKERS!

¡VALIENTES CREADORAS DE LA HISTORIA!

11 Women from Latin America who changed the World

11 Mujeres de Latinoamérica que cambiaron el mundo

To all the women in this book that have changed the world with their magic. - NR

A esas mujeres que abrieron el camino, en especial a mi mamá y mi abuela.- JL

Written by: Naibe Reynoso   Illustrations by: Jone Leal   Translated by Gabriella Aldeman

Text and Illustration Copyright© 2021 by Con Todo Press

ISBN: 978-1-7362744-3-9 (Hardcover)
ISBN: 978-1-7362744-0-8 (Paperback)
ISBN: 978-1-7362744-2-2 (Ebook)

Publisher's Cataloging-in-Publication data

Names: Reynoso, Naibe, author. | Leal, Jone, illustrator. | Aldeman, Gabriella, translator.
Title: Courageous history makers! : 11 women from Latin America who changed the world | ¡Valientes creadoras de la historia! : 11 mujeres de Latinoamérica que cambiaron el mundo / written by: Naibe Reynoso ; illustrated by: Jone Leal ; translated by: Gabriella Aldeman.
Series: Little Biographies for Bright Minds
Description: Includes bibliographical references | Los Angeles, CA: Con Todo Press, 2021.
Identifiers: LCCN: 2021902331
ISBN: 978-1-7362744-3-9 (Hardcover) | 978-1-7362744-0-8 (pbk.) | 978-1-7362744-2-2 (e-book)

Subjects: LCSH Women--Latin America--Biography--Juvenile literature. | Hispanic American women--Biography--Juvenile literature. | Latinos (U.S.)--Biography--Juvenile literature. | Women--United States--Biography--Juvenile literature. | CYAC Women--Latin America--Biography. | Latin Americans--Biography. | Latinos (U.S.)--Biography. | Women--United States--Biography. | BISAC BIOGRAPHY & AUTOBIOGRAPHY / Cultural, Ethnic & Regional / Hispanic & Latino | BIOGRAPHY & AUTOBIOGRAPHY / Women

Classification: LCC CT3290 R49 2021 | DDC 920.72--dc23

CON TODO PRESS BOOKS

CON TODO
PRESS

contodopress.com

All notations of errors or omissions should be emailed to the address below.

For bulk orders contact: contodopress@gmail.com

NAIBE REYNOSO Author

Naibe Reynoso is a Mexican-American multi-Emmy award-winning journalist with over two decades of career experience. Her work has been seen in CNN Español, France 24, Reelz Channel, Univision, Telemundo/KWHY, and Fox News Latino to name a few. Her first children's book was "Be Bold, Be Brave: 11 Latinas who made U.S. History." She graduated from UCLA with a degree in Sociology, and a double concentration in Psychology and Chicano Studies. She lives in her native, Los Angeles, California with her teenage daughter, young son and husband Jeff. To learn more about the author, go to naibereynoso.com or follow her on Instagram @naibereynoso

Jone Leal- Illustrator

Jone Leal, also known as "jonewho" is a Venezuelan illustrator who loves to work with children's book illustrations and women empowerment. She has over 5 years of experience in the area. When she's not drawing, you can find her sewing while listening to her favorite music. She also illustrated "Be Bold! Be Brave! 11 Latinas who made U.S. History." To see more of her work visit jonewho.com or follow her on Instagram @jonewho

Frida Kahlo fue una artista mexicana que pintaba sobre su cultura y sociedad.
Conocida por sus autorretratos, creó cuadros de una amplia variedad.

Era atrevida en su estilo y técnica e imaginativa de personalidad.
Frida rompió barreras y es hoy un símbolo del feminismo y latinidad.

Su trabajo ha estado en los mejores museos, como el Louvre en París, Francia.
Miles desean ver su arte de cerca y para admirarlo viajan grandes distancias.

FRIDA KAHLO
Mexican Painter

Frida Kahlo was an artist whose work reflected Mexican culture and society.
Well-known for her self-portraits, she created paintings of a wide variety.

She was daring and imaginative in her personality, style and technique.
Frida broke many barriers for women; she was courageous and unique.

Her work was shown in famous museums like the Louvre in Paris, France.
Millions wish to see her art up close, if only for a glance.

Viridiana Álvarez vio las montañas más grandes del mundo y las quiso escalar.
Las subió en tiempo récord con su tenacidad ejemplar.

Las cimas del Everest, K2 y monte Kangchenjunga conquistó.
Con propósito y valentía, hasta el cielo tocó.

Viridiana es alpinista y escala paso a paso con perseverancia.
Tú también puedes ser imparable y viajar cualquier distancia.

VIRIDIANA ÁLVAREZ
Mountaineer

Viridiana Álvarez set her sights on mountains to climb!
With tenacity she reached her goal, scaling the tallest ones in record time.

From Mount Kangchenjunga in Nepal, to Mount Everest and K2,
she reached the tops of each peak, and with courage so can you!

Viridiana is a mountaineer and climbs with bravery and persistence!
You too can be unstoppable and travel any distance.

Nacida en Ecuador en 1905, Hermelinda Urvina soñaba con conquistar el cielo.
Con coraje y valentía, logró su meta y pronto tomó vuelo.

Incluso cuando había barreras, siguió su pasión por la aviación.
Fue la primera mujer piloto de América del Sur. ¡Su historia es una inspiración!

Hermelinda, junto a Amelia Earhart, fundaron una organización
de pilotos femenina.
Quería ayudar a otras como ella e inspirar a toda latina.

HERMELINDA URVINA
Pilot

Born in Ecuador in 1905, Hermelinda Urvina had the dream to one day fly.
With plenty of grit and bravery, she was soon soaring in the sky!

Despite so many barriers, she followed her passion for aviation,
and became the first South American female pilot! What an inspiration!

Hermelinda was a co-founder of the Ninety-Nines, a female pilot organization.
She wanted to help other women pursue their dreams
and inspire new generations.

Nacida en Colombia, Caterine Ibargüen pronto fue mundialmente reconocida.
Campeona en salto y atletismo, esta deportista no se da por vencida.

Es dedicada y fuerte. ¡Cómo corre en el asfalto!
Caterine es poderosa y competitiva al dominar el triple salto.

Sobresale en competencias internacionales y en las Olimpiadas ganó el oro.
¡Ibargüen es una campeona mundial y, para el deporte, un gran tesoro!

CATERINE IBARGÜEN
Athlete / Olympic Gold Medalist

Born in Colombia, Caterine Ibargüen's talents were soon revealed.
She became a world-class athlete, a champion of track and field.

She's dedicated, competitive, powerful and strong!
She dominates the triple jump! Her jump is really long!

She's won international contests, and took gold in the Olympic Games.
Ibargüen is a worldwide champion! She's earned global fame!

Rigoberta Menchú nació en Guatemala, de ascendencia maya.
Defiende los derechos indígenas y siempre enfrenta cualquier batalla.

Hasta se postuló para la presidencia, Rigoberta no se pone limitaciones.
Es una activista dedicada a las causas indígenas de Guatemala y sus poblaciones.

Ganó el Premio Nobel por su activismo que comenzó de adolescente.
¡Nunca eres demasiado joven para usar tu voz, y hablar por tu gente!

RIGOBERTA MENCHÚ
Activist / Nobel Peace Prize Winner

Rigoberta Menchú was born in Guatemala, of K'iche, Mayan descent.
She's a defender of indigenous rights—that's the cause she represents.

Rigoberta ran for president; she has no self-limitations.
She's a dedicated activist for Guatemala's indigenous populations.

She's a Nobel Prize recipient and was an activist from a young age.
It's never too early to use your voice to be heard on the global stage.

Celia Cruz cantó por todo el mundo; era famosa en cada lugar.
Su música y carisma tropical ponían a todos a bailar.

Interpretó ritmos afrocubanos como guaracha, rumba, bolero y son.
Un ícono de la música latina, Celia cantaba con sazón.

La Reina de la Salsa, conocida por su alegría,
ganó Grammys, fama mundial y un público que la quería.

CELIA CRUZ
Musical Icon

Celia Cruz traveled 'round the world so many could enjoy
her music and warm spirit that to others brought such joy.

She mastered Afro-Cuban music styles
like guaracha, rumba, bolero, and son.
Her music is unique and everlasting, like her there's only one!

Known as the "Queen of Salsa," she was bold in voice and style.
Most importantly she gave the gift of happiness!
She always wore a smile.

Teresa Carreño fue una niña prodigio, genio en el piano.
Nacida en Venezuela en 1853, también fue compositora, directora y soprano.

Desde pequeña le apasionó la música y mostró talento y habilidad.
Rompió muchas barreras en su industria sin importar género o edad.

Sus dedos bailaban sobre el piano creando melodías y bellos sonidos.
¡A los nueve años tocó para el presidente Lincoln en la Casa Blanca
de Estados Unidos!

TERESA CARREÑO
Pianist

Teresa Carreño was a child prodigy known as the "valkyrie of the piano."
Born in Venezuela in 1853, she was also a composer, conductor and soprano!

From a young age she loved music for its magnificence and splendor.
Teresa broke through many barriers for her age and gender.

Her fingers danced on the piano;
she played melodies angelic and divine.
She performed for President Lincoln
in the White House at age nine!

Aracely Quispe es la primera latina en liderar tres misiones espaciales de la NASA.
Oriunda de Marripón, Perú, con tenacidad sus sueños siempre alcanza.

Es ingeniera, científica y estudió cómo se derriten los glaciares.
También es atleta y cinta negra, sobresale en las artes marciales.

Aracely inspira a jóvenes a estudiar tecnología, ingeniería, matemáticas y ciencia.
Es oradora, pionera y un tesoro humano por su excelencia.

ARACELY QUISPE
NASA Engineer

Aracely Quispe is the first Latina to command three NASA space missions!
Born in Marripón, Peru, she is proud of her culture and its traditions!

She is an engineer and studied science,
specializing in glaciers and why they melt.
She's also an athlete, a karate pro,
and even earned a black belt!

Aracely inspires young girls to pursue careers in STEM.
A speaker and a trailblazer, she is a human gem!

Nacida en Chile, Gabriela Mistral fue una de las grandes poetas del continente.
También era maestra y diplomática. ¡Fue excepcionalmente inteligente!

Sus poesías son mundialmente reconocidas; sus palabras, siempre sabias.
Gabriela ganó un Premio Nobel por ser una gran voz literaria.

Para ser como Gabriela, una visionaria de importantes habilidades,
lee libros, estudia y verás que hay múltiples posibilidades.

GABRIELA MISTRAL
Poet / Nobel Prize in Literature Recipient

Born in Chile, Gabriela Mistral wrote poems from the heart.
She was also a teacher and diplomat; she was exceptionally smart!

Her poetries are world-renowned, her words are very wise.
Gabriela Mistral won many awards, including a Nobel Prize!

Like Gabriela, find your passion and have confidence in your abilities.
Your potential has no bounds; there are endless possibilities!

Prudencia Ayala, nacida en El Salvador, luchó por los derechos de la mujer.
Sabía que las niñas merecían respeto y llegarían a ser líderes con poder.

Fue escritora, periodista y política de su nación.
Y en 1931 hizo historia. A esto pongan atención:

¡Fue la primera mujer latina en postularse para ser presidente!
Como Prudencia, piensa en grande, y lograrás lo que tengas en mente.

PRUDENICA AYALA
Writer/Social Activist

Born in El Salvador, Prudencia Ayala promoted women's rights.
She was humble and determined, and her vision reached great heights.

Writing was her passion, until politics caught her attention.
In 1931 she made history for an important thing to mention...

She was the first Latin American woman to run as a presidential nominee.
Think big like Prudencia and there's no limit to what you can be!

Laura Chinchilla fue presidente de Costa Rica; lideró con valentía esa nación.
Impulsó políticas para proteger el mar, el medioambiente,
y apoyó la conservación.

Es defensora de los derechos de la mujer y promotora
de la tecnología y la educación.
Tiene tres doctorados honorarios. ¡Laura es una inspiración!

Si, como Laura, quieres ser una líder con grandes responsabilidades,
¡cree en ti misma!, ¡sé valiente! y confía en tus propias habilidades.

LAURA CHINCHILLA
Former President of Costa Rica

Laura Chinchilla led her country with courage and determination.
As President of Costa Rica, she promoted women's rights,
technology, and education,

She's an advocate for the environment,
supporting land and marine conservation,
and holds three honorary doctorate degrees. She's an inspiration!

If you want to be a leader like Laura with big responsibilities,
be brave, have confidence and always trust in your abilities.

YOU / TÚ

All these women are phenomenal, unique in their own way.
But look at your OWN reflection and you'll see brilliance on display!

Whether you're from a tropical island or the mountains of Peru
YOU are amazing, brilliant and terrific, just for being YOU!

What makes you different makes you EXCEPTIONAL and great!
There are no limits to your future and the things YOU can create!

Estas mujeres audaces hicieron historia a su manera.
¡Ahora mira tu PROPIO reflejo y podrás ver lo que te espera!

Ya seas de una isla tropical o de las montañas de Perú,
eres increíble, brillante y fabulosa, ¡solo por ser TÚ!

¡Lo que te hace diferente, te hace EXCEPCIONAL y singular!
¡No hay límites para tu futuro ni las cosas que puedes lograr!

FRIDA KHALO is a Mexican artist born in 1907 in Mexico City. Her home, known as the Blue House, is now a museum holding dozens of her pieces. She is of Hungarian, German, and Indigenous Oaxacan descent. At six years old, she contracted polio. At eighteen years old, she was in a serious bus accident and suffered severe injuries, resulting in Kahlo having to be put in a full-body cast. Her paintings are now worth millions. Frida Khalo's work is the most expensive of any Latin American artist. Khalo passed away at only 47 years old.

VIRIDIANA ALVAREZ is a record-breaking Mexican mountain climber. As of 2020, she holds the Guinness World Record for climbing the three highest mountains in the world in record-breaking time (Mount Everest in Nepal/China; K2 in Pakistan/China, and Kanchenjunga in Nepal/India). She is the first Latina to conquer the world's second tallest mountain (K2) and the first woman in North America to climb the four tallest mountains in the world (Everest, K2, Kanchenjunga, and Lhotse).

HERMELINDA URVINA MAYORGA was born in 1905 in Ambato, Ecuador. She was the first South American female to become an officially licensed pilot. Urvina was an early member of the Ninety-Nines, an organization for female pilots that Amelia Earhart helped create. According to Legacy.com, Urvina also enjoyed other extreme sports like boating and snowmobiling. She has been named "one of the ten most influential women of the millennium" by an Ecuadorian newspaper, *El Comercio*. Hermelinda lived to be 103 years old!

CATERINE IBARGÜEN is a Colombian Olympic gold medalist. She was born in 1984 in Apartadó, Colombia. Ibargüen represented Colombia at 3 Olympic Games: Athens 2004, London 2012 (silver medal winner), and Rio 2016 (gold medal winner). She is known for competing in the high jump, long jump, and triple jump. She has set Colombian and world records. She is an IAAF World Champion and was named 2018 IAAF Female Athlete of the Year.

RIGOBERTA MENCHÚ is a Mayan activist. She was born in Laj Chimel, Guatemala, in 1959. She was a member of the United Peasant Committee. In 1983 she wrote a biography called *I, Rigoberta Menchú: An Indian Woman in Guatemala*. In 1992, Rigoberta received the Nobel Peace Prize for her social justice work for the Indigenous community. She started a foundation called Menchú Tum Foundation (FRMT) to support Mayan communities. In 2007 she ran for President of Guatemala. She was the first Indigenous person to begin and lead a political party in Guatemala.

CELIA CRUZ was born in Cuba in 1925. In 1950, she joined *La Sonora Matancera*, becoming the orchestra's first Black lead singer. She is known as "The Queen of Salsa," earning 23 Gold Records, 3 Grammy Awards, 4 Latin Grammy Awards, and a star on the Hollywood Walk of Fame. She was also awarded the American National Medal of the Arts by President Bill Clinton. Cruz is in the Billboard Latin Music Hall of Fame, the International Latin Music Hall of Fame, and was awarded the Grammy's Lifetime Achievement Award. She holds honorary doctorates from Yale University and the University of Miami. Celia's legacy continues through the Celia Cruz Foundation.

TERESA CARREÑO was born in 1853 in Caracas, Venezuela. She is a pianist, composer, and opera singer. She learned to play the piano at age six and was known as a child prodigy. She performed for President Abraham Lincoln and President Woodrow Wilson at the White House. She toured throughout the U.S., Venezuela, Cuba, and Europe. She most famously composed the national anthem of Venezuela.

ARACELY QUISPE is a Peruvian STEM professional and NASA engineer. She is from Morropón, Peru. She earned a master's degree in Astronautical Engineering from Capitol Technology University, a master's degree in Geospatial Engineering from the University of Maryland, and a doctorate degree in Science from Capitol Technology University. She is known as the first Latina to lead three missions at NASA. She is a professor at Capitol Technology University. She also holds a black belt degree in karate!

PRUDENCIA AYALA is an Indigenous Salvadorian feminist icon born in 1885. Ayala is a self-taught political expert as she did not complete elementary school because of her family's inability to afford proper schooling. She is known for advocating for the poor and working-class, the Indigenous community, and women through journalism. In 1921, she published her first book, *Escible, Adventures of a Trip to Guatemala,* and later published various other political pieces. She eventually founded the newspaper *Redención Femenina,* which highlights women's and worker's rights. In 1930, Ayala became the first woman to attempt to run for President of El Salvador, even though the Salvadoran legislation did not recognize women's right to vote.

GABRIELA MISTRAL is a Chilean scholar, poet, and diplomat. She was born in 1889 in Vicuña, Chile. She started as a public school teacher and later gained higher ranking roles in developing different school systems of Latin America. In 1922, she worked with Mexico's president in pioneering Mexico's first public school system. She is best known for her poetry. In 1945, Mistral became the first Latin American and fifth woman to receive the Nobel Prize in Literature. By 1946, she became a diplomatic delegate for the United Nations, where she created the "Appeal for Children," which inspired the beginning of UNICEF.

LAURA CHINCHILLA, the first female president of Costa Rica, was born in San Jose, Costa Rica, in 1959. She was elected in 2010 and served until 2014. She holds the title of the sixth female president in Latin America. She also served as Costa Rica's vice president and as a congresswoman. She earned her undergraduate degree in Political Sciences from Universidad de Costa Rica and a master's degree in Public Policy from Georgetown University. She also holds Honorary Doctorates from the University for Peace of the United Nations and Kyoto University of Foreign Studies.

Bibliography

FRIDA KHALO

https://www.fridakahlo.org/
https://www.museofridakahlo.org.mx/en/frida-kahlo-en/#back-top
https://www.smithsonianmag.com/arts-culture/frida-kahlo-70745811/?page=2
https://artsandculture.google.com/exhibit/frida-kahlo-¡viva-la-vida/BwJSiccgMhf8LA

VIRIDIANA ÁLVAREZ

https://www.cnn.com/travel/article/guinness-world-records-mountaineer-winner-viridiana-lvarez-chvez/index.html
https://www.guinnessworldrecords.com/
https://www.travelandleisure.com/travel-news/viridiana-alvarez-chavez-latina-mountaineer-guinness-world-record-everest
https://www.viridianaalvarez.com/

HERMELINDA URVINA

https://peoplepill.com/people/hermelinda-urvina/
https://www.legacy.com/obituaries/thestar/obituary.aspx?n=hermelinda-urbina-mayorga-de-briones&pid=117801131
https://www.ninety-nines.org/our-history.htm

CATERINE IBARGÜEN

https://www.globalsportscommunication.nl/athletes/most-successful-athletes/EN11866-Caterine-Ibarg%C3%BCen.aspx
https://www.olympic.org/caterine-ibarguen

RIGOBERTA MENCHÚ

https://nobelwomensinitiative.org/laureate/rigoberta-menchu-tum/
https://www.nobelprize.org/prizes/peace/1992/tum/biographical/
https://www.tolerance.org/classroom-resources/texts/rigoberta-menchu

CELIA CRUZ

https://celiacruz.com/biography/
https://www.npr.org/2018/02/13/584004511/celia-cruzs-son-con-guaguanc-and-the-bridge-to-fame-in-exile
https://www.grammy.com/grammys/artists/celia-cruz/1461
https://celiacruzfoundation.com

TERESA CARREÑO

https://hispanicsociety.org/program/concert-series/hispanic-women-composers-i-am-carreno-the-extraordinary-life-of-teresa-carreno-1853-1917/
https://www.independent.co.uk/arts-entertainment/music/teresa-carreno-music-death-google-doodle-composer-piano-venezuela-who-facts-a8695341.html
https://www.google.com/doodles/teresa-carrenos-165th-birthday
https://www.squiltmusic.com/blogs/news/teresa-carreno

ARACELY QUISPE

https://themazatlanpost.com/2019/12/14/aracely-quispe-first-latina-woman-to-command-three-missions-in-nasa/
https://andina.pe/ingles/noticia-aracely-quispe-pride-and-lead-of-peruvian-who-conquered-nasa-772655.aspx
https://aracelyquispeneira.com/biografia/

GABRIELA MISTRAL

https://www.nobelprize.org/prizes/literature/1945/mistral/biographical/
https://www.gabrielamistralfoundation.org
https://www.poetryfoundation.org/poets/gabriela-mistral

PRUDENCIA AYALA

https://www.americasquarterly.org/article/she-dared-to-run-the-unlikely-story-of-prudencia-ayala/
https://pioneeringwomen.org/?p=100
https://www.academia.edu/43339555/Biographical_data_of_Prudencia_Ayala

LAURA CHINCHILLA

https://politics.georgetown.edu/profile/laura-chinchilla/
https://www.olympic.org/ms-laura-chinchilla
https://ticotimes.net/2014/05/07/laura-chinchillas-environmental-report-card
https://kids.kiddle.co/Laura_Chinchilla

CON TODO PRESS BOOKS

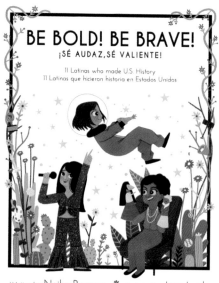

BE BOLD! BE BRAVE!
¡SÉ AUDAZ, SÉ VALIENTE!
11 Latinas who made U.S. History
11 Latinas que hicieron historia en Estados Unidos

Written by: Naibe Reynoso • Illustrated by: Jone Leal

FEARLESS TRAILBLAZERS
PIONEROS AUDACES
11 Latinos who made U.S. History
11 Latinos que hicieron historia en Estados Unidos

Written by: Naibe Reynoso • Illustrated by: Jone Leal

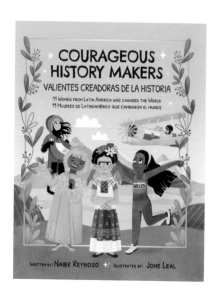

COURAGEOUS HISTORY MAKERS
VALIENTES CREADORAS DE LA HISTORIA
11 Women from Latin America who changed the World
11 Mujeres de Latinoamérica que cambiaron el mundo

Written by: Naibe Reynoso • Illustrated by: Jone Leal

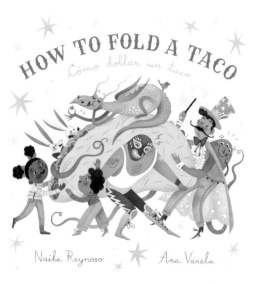

HOW TO FOLD A TACO
Cómo doblar un taco

Naibe Reynoso • Ana Varela

BE BOLD! BE BRAVE!
¡SÉ AUDAZ, SÉ VALIENTE!
CHIQUITOS
11 Latinas who made U.S. History

Naibe Reynoso & Jone Leal

CON TODO
PRESS

CONTODOPRESS.COM